Leaving

Cees Nooteboom

Leaving

A Poem from the Time of the Virus

Translated by David Colmer

With Drawings by Max Neumann

Seagull
BOOKS

LONDON NEW YORK CALCUTTA

Seagull Books, 2021

Original poems © Cees Nooteboom
Original drawings © Max Neumann
This compilation © Seagull Books, 2021
English translation © David Colmer, 2021

First published in English translation by Seagull Books, 2021

ISBN 978 0 8574 2 883 7

British Library Cataloguing-in-Publication Data
A catalogue record for this book is available from the British Library

Typeset by Seagull Books, Calcutta, India
Printed and bound by Hyam Enterprises, Calcutta, India

in memoriam
Emilio de Balanzó
Hans Roters, amigos isleños

1

1

The end of the end, the man in the winter garden
asked himself, what could that be?
If nothing else, he thought, not any kind of sorrow.
He looked outside and saw a cloud that looked

like a cloud, as grey as lead, too heavy
for every balance, the bare fig against the wall
with the thousand-year-old stones,
the geese next door, their disapproval,

the way the night needed to be set right,
the grammar of expropriation, nobody
themselves anymore, not a single apparition,
withdrawal after defeat

but no destination.

2

He'd seen that in the war, defeated soldiers
in retreat, frightened, dirty, the mouths
that sang so heartily when they marched in
now closed. They had sung of triumph,

their tiny lives had suddenly expanded,
fitted with new futures, victims, others
to maltreat, the back of the mirror,
now turned again, the fate of destiny.

He remembered it well, the humbled backs
he saw again now. He was no army but felt
the lesson like a rabbit feels the hunter's blow,
imposed without mercy and

all over.

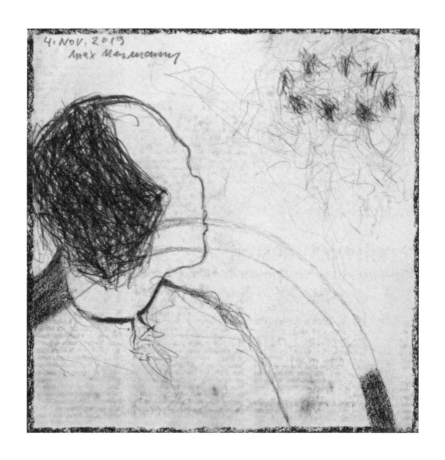

3

The war that never stopped coming back,
a guest who's known to all, a toothless
kiss, the language of intimate betrayal
around him now again, remembering a past

he couldn't share with anyone. His father,
a man in a dinner suit leaning on the railing
of the boulevard, his mother alongside the future
deceased, already wrapped in the time to come,

and he himself still hidden, the world a cloud
without rules, and behind his parents the sea,
the warning no one wanted to hear, always
the same, the sound of indrawn breath,

devouring so much.

4

What he liked most was the gibbering
of philosophers, alone again now in his room,
the other gone, the cloud turned back to night,
the geese quiet, the danger past. Or was it?

Disguised in the joy of night, the quiet surrounds
the house, letting him tune his ear to the voices
from before: gibberish as wisdom—many heads
sprung up without necks and arms wandered

bare and bereft of shoulders, eyes strayed
up and down in want of foreheads, solitary
limbs wandered, apparitions, a phantasmagoria
woven from evil stories, but please

take a seat.

27.04. 2019

5

Still marked by that same war,
he had dreamt his way into a world
that was not the world, rediscovering
himself among others as a stranger,

someone with wings, but no talons,
transparent, in love with shells
and stones, a leaf on the wind, to
and fro, surrounded by poems,

never far from the sea. Living behind the masks
were the others, drowned in their mirrors,
buzzing softly within their own thoughts,
halls of inconceivable simplicity but no

place anywhere.

6

The poet sleeps. This is the hour of the gardener.
Dead leaves, the ground black and wet, cactus
cradled in its thorns, son
of the storm. In a year the flower

the months await will come, child
of a single hour and a colour in keeping with that,
the purple of birth and grief. In this garden, duration
has no predicate, time no imperative.

This is his family, green and tenacious,
never afraid of the end, their silence
the poem that spells out their essence.
Whimpering at the garden gate is the world, the

fuss of a newspaper.

22.Okt 2013   Max Mannheimer

7

My strange domain. My friends who don't
have mouths. All points and angular arms,
they guard the walls and wait with me for words
to come so I can slot them in

to what will become a form. I walked
the world to get here. They are
the destination I didn't know.
Their names are strange and melodious,

their forms serrated, they know much more
than me, they relate themselves
in their forms but stay within them,
our conversation consists of my looking,

poem of the eye.

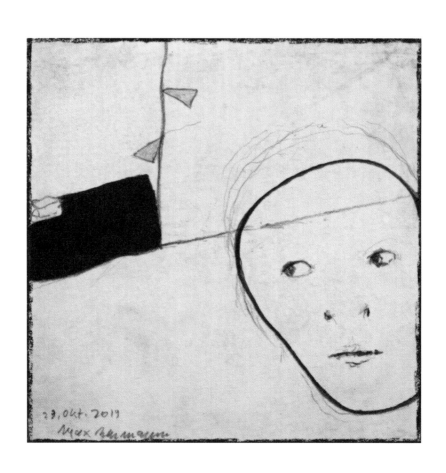

8

And once again those enduring images appear,
well-dressed people setting out on a journey,
looking for a compartment that doesn't exist,
next stop Armageddon, a continent

where time does not apply. Uniforms too
with different stars, boots shining
on the ice of death. There is nothing
mysterious about any of this.

Everyone out! Among them the girl
in the door opening, last glance at the world,
a platform with a man in grey,
a tree in the distance

sees everything.

9

Hear the music but not the words,
a dance step but nobody there.
A poem without a reader.
Time without numbers.

How many riddles can you bear?
The friend who died but could no longer talk,
the other friend who in his final bed
traced a circle with his hands

and meant travel. That was a goodbye
and I understood, it was up to me
to keep travelling, circling the globe
until it brought me back to him again,

or him to me, a futile promise.

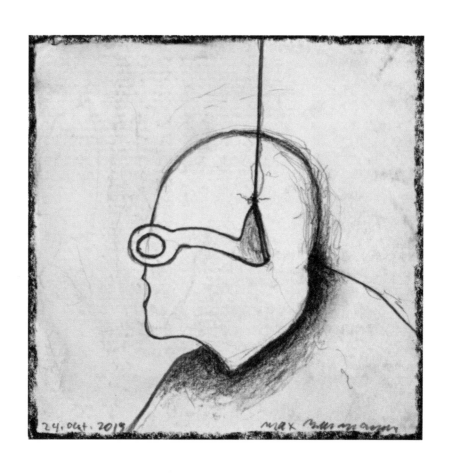

24. Okt. 2019   Max Ballmann

10

Him and me, the confusing twins?
summer garden, winter garden, war
and later, now they were together
looking at the heads.

The procession
that blended into their dreams,
appearing to my me's him,
to my him's me,

memories for company,
the ongoing riddle that passed them both
with a many-footed rush
on its way to a battle

in the mirror.

31.Okt. 2019   max mem m

11

I saw heads, countless heads,
field marshals, lovers, travellers
from star to star. Each head its
own story, hidden in the folds

of the brain, alongside narrow streams
of blood, reeds on the banks, secret
landscapes no one can reach,
except for a lonely traveller,

who will hear everything, concealed
thoughts, desires. That lonely traveller
was me, and alone on the water
I wrote down what I saw, what I heard

head after head.

2

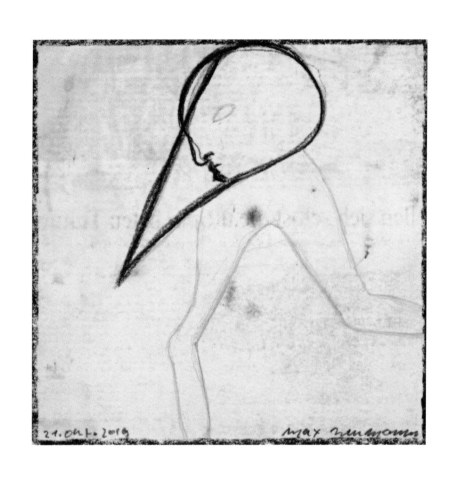

21. Okt. 2019   Max Neumann

1

Light between the images, the man in the
winter garden, the heron, the wanderer,
the man searching for the maker in the confusing
illusion leans back,

distance from all horror,
catches his breath, not fleeing but staying.
This must be borne, it's part
of the task. He looks at the heads,

they are part of his being, he knows them
from previous centuries, their bloodlust,
their delusion. The numbered king
who had his brother murdered

because of a woman.

2

The animal that tried to think,
the girl from thousands of years
ago with hair of flax, just
found. The rows never

end. He can't list them image
by image, but no matter what he asks
about the forms, shadows and almost
invisible mouths, the menace

of the names and numbers, the answer stays
as empty. Does he want to know them?
They frighten him. Does he need to know them,
do they have the knowledge he once sought,

is he free to go?

3

How many lives go into a life?
How often is the same head someone else?
Does the murderer push past the lover
or make up another riddle?

He made up fairy tales, imagining
a life for each head, studying them when they
weren't looking. Sopranos sang
in the distance while he peered at them.

The heads he had made that
didn't want to know him, strangers,
companions in adversity from another existence,
he didn't want to share anything with them

except the fear.

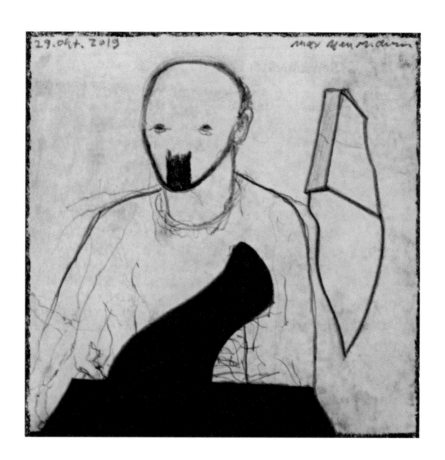

4

At times deceptively normal like the mother
of a dead soldier, then a spectre beside
a wreck, the unreal has a cast
of thousands, dream, a malevolent

imagination, a transparent body menaced
by the executioner's helper, a half-
open mouth with something left
to say, a dark haze

of ominous scratches isolates a man or
a woman's face, angular shapes
almost conceal another. Who are
these people, from which slums did they creep

without names?

5

No love here, only violence,
loneliness, melancholy, the form
of an animal, a man accompanied by
his guillotine, a child without a mouth.

Who are these creatures, deadened,
malicious, fearful, a vision of a
perilous world, wandering between the
white and the black of night,

between fate and destiny
in a country no one knows
except the lonely maker
they do not speak to

because nobody knows him.

6

A ship founders right through a face,
a rotting source, a three-master
through closed eyes, who
is the creator?

An inverted paradise full
of monsters that look like us, a
blank, gnawed face with a
shrub on her back. Heads,

together with mine in the mirror
without asking why
or what I am doing here, corpses that move
to the rhythm of a dance step, carnival

of fear.

8. Nov. 2017   Max Meyruchen

7

Stop! Look at your heads,
they are people for all your disbelief.
An evolutionary backstreet, hair
sprouting from throats.

Was there a prescribed measure?
But how do the executioner,
the swindler, the poetaster
fit into it? The half face on

an almost non-existent body,
the wingless insect that wrote
a book, the invented genius
who sells his vomit in a job lot

with his soul?

8. Nov. 2019   Max Meumeyer

8

What is it like when a snake
becomes human, when vertebrae
seize power, when an egg stares at you
with gaping eyes?

These are lessons in the clearest
doom, the back of the
possible, where nothing is
built or repaired, this

is quicksand portrayed,
a poem about the evil
we can't close our eyes to
because bearing it

is part of it all.

10. Nov. 2019   Max Beckmann

9

You wanted to live, didn't you?
Did you only want gold, the blue
of the sky, love, the sun?
Nothing here is free, gather

death in all its manifestations,
the pain, the scream, the cruel
embrace, the kiss of deliberate
betrayal.

Life, the song of songs? Sure,
but underneath there is that other truth,
the truth of night and fog,
the test that lasts

until the end.

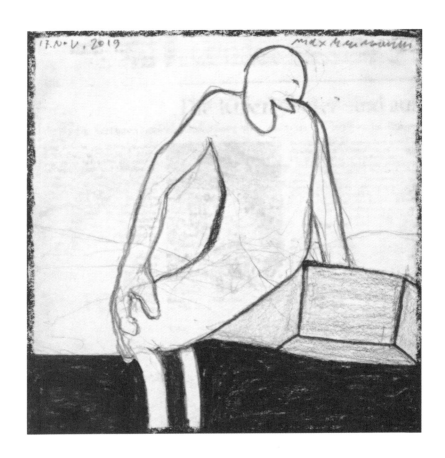

10

Who is saying all this, which voice is calling
the man in his lonely room, from which antiquity
is someone trying to speak of struggle
or mutilation? Isn't his own day

enough? All repetition, all read
in books, reinvented pain, cleavers
under words, sacrifice under skies
that are always the same, nothing new made-up.

He knows, everything comes past one last time
before the end, before he's free to go and
who knows maybe laugh like an orphan in the dark
clinging to words of poetry.

Nothing will be left undone.

13. Nov. 2019   max hillmann

11

Don't walk away. Stay with this gentle
view of a summer's evening, peace,
a conversation on the water, whispering,
murmuring that washes away

disaster. He hears the horse
in the meadow, a last bird on the wing,
don't get up, dispel the danger,
don't be afraid of the shape

of the face without eyes,
the woman with hair of rope,
the disembodied mouth,
don't let them enter the sleep

that is yours.

3

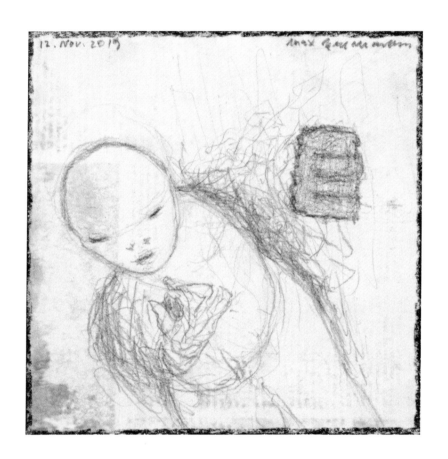

1

On a György Kurtág CD I saw a stone
with two ears. Not on the sides, but next to each other
in relief. In the middle of an empty surface.
It looks old, but the clear photo

provides no explanation. Is the stone listening,
does it hear when I ask what it means?
I keep quiet. I want to know what it hears and
hear silence. Then I softly hum a dream

that the stone starts to move. But the stone
remains as still and silent as a stone. Behind
the right ear a chip is missing. Did it
hear the crack, at least? But it won't even

tell me that.

2

What was I trying to say in those craggy lines,
in rhymes that collide with their likeness,
the forgotten measured, the temporary triumph
of music? Who would want to dance

to that? Closed figures from a
prophecy, a truth as art.
Try that in the face of the stars that
observe the worst,

the note of infinite sorrow
rising from victims.
The pawned vision of the many,
a depraved image of parlando,

the frock of the news.

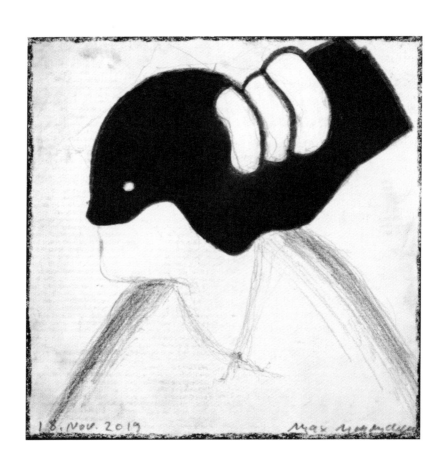

18. Nov. 2019   Max Mannheimer

3

What kind of noise does Earth make
in the house of space? Buzzing, humming,
stuttering, weeping its way without ever
arriving. All dreamed up by a who

or a what with an army of helpers,
a honeyed tongue as well to squash
sorrow, a future promised
and refused while time was being

counted. How long did he count and consider
in his invented second, never was it
about him, he had read everything
the best had written

in invisible ink.

15. Nov. 2019   Max Neumann

4

Sorrow has only one dimension
in which everything is hidden, a never
forgotten glance, grief and ecstasy, moments
of love and friendship, a colourful

marble rolling slowly over
the edge of the playground
where nothing is preserved. Altogether,
once a life. What had you hoped

to preserve? The sound of a voice,
the memory of a shoulder, a
hand, the colour of her eyes, the smell
of a body, faded

forever?

18. Nov. 2019

5

I was walking on the longest road, the road
that doesn't go anywhere. Caverns, an empty landscape
the colour of sand and straw. There were others
with me, friends, brothers, lovers

and they kept saying goodbye, turning left
or right, disappearing like ghosts,
each alone in their solitude. They didn't look back, they
knew where they were going, they traced straight lines

through emptiness. I saw them go, the people
of my life, walking slowly out of my and
their existence. I thought about them as long
as I could see them, listening for the sound of their far voices,

made of air.

22. Nov, 2019   Max Beckmann

6

Silence as a hymn, I've never heard
nothingness like this before, contradiction
surrounds me, an organ,
no keys, a song

whose sound has been sealed,
the cities, the deserts of my
life wither in this music
without notes, already almost

absent, my being still hesitates,
wanting to turn back, but it knows,
nobody's there anymore, the light
moving beside me is

all I have.

7

Now the bird too is disappearing with slow
flaps of its wings, I hear them, an infinite
andante. It flies over what is
still visible of the road,

a trail now of crushed shells
and sandy grit. A last
reminder of the sea and of
water, once my home.

My kind is born of water, we
were sea creatures, seeded
by the stars, scattered over water
to become the form we

know.

8

Creatures that walk upright,
estranged from their origin,
strangers that think
and pay the price.

We have left the others
behind in the bliss
of innocence, brothers
and sisters who do not know

their end, deck themselves out
as creation with claws
and colours, horns and scales,
tails and shells

but no names.

9

Now my feet are counting the road, I know,
looking back is not allowed. My steps measure time,
a dark and peerless poem, a beat
that can't be slowed. I do my best

to still make out all kinds of things the way
I always have. High overhead still, the bird
that pretended to follow me, a last
companion who knew where I was going,

who knew my road. So many roads
I've wandered, always in search of something
that could only lie ahead and when I saw it
at last, disappeared like a mirage

or appeared as a poem.

10

Someone there is rising to her feet,
a final figure moving away,
the only one of my existence,
I watch her go.

I feel my longing
leaving me, this wasn't meant to be
and now it's happened, exit
she who made it

possible. Disappearing
with her, the words
of who I was
the last part

of the road.

11

Now silence is
the rest of the distance
without memory
no life.

I hear my steps
no more,
what surrounds me
is hidden.

Blind I walk on, a grey dog
in the cold. This must be it,
the place I say goodbye to my self
and slowly become

no one.

———

San Luis, November 2019

Hofgut Missen, April 2020

AFTERWORD

How does a volume of poetry arise? You start in a garden describing Mediterranean plants, but what emerges are thoughts of the war, images from a distant past that has never disappeared.

And then the poem takes another turn: someone suddenly appears or, rather, intervenes, you are given a folder of drawings that strangely, and perhaps only for you, echo a pre-Socratic text by Empedocles you had noted earlier, before the poem was there, but can no longer access because of the pandemic; and because poetry sometimes does as it pleases, the heads depicted in these drawings connect mysteriously with those lines by Empedocles in the fourth poem in the first series, interrupting the meditation, and in the eleventh poem in the first series, they send the poem in a new direction. Meanwhile you have arrived in another country yourself, but the mysterious virus that is suddenly ruling the world has changed life here, too, and it would be strange if the poem ignored all that. In the large city where you temporarily find yourself, the wide streets are empty, you see a poster that says *does the hereafter start here.* Now it seems as if reality itself wants to help write the poem. You withdraw to quiet surroundings, northern landscapes, the poem takes you by the hand again and returns to those first lines written months ago in a winter garden somewhere else, *the end of the end, what could that be?*

Hofgut Missen
May 2020

The lines of Empedocles (I.4, lines 7 to 10) are quoted from John Burnet's *Early Greek Philosophy*, first published in 1892.

*

The drawings by Max Neumann featured in this volume were created between 21 October and 25 November 2019. They are all untitled, mixed-media-on-paper works, measuring 20 cm x 20 cm.